21105998-

A DAY *in the* LIFE *of*
A VICTORIAN STREET SELLER

Richard Wood
Illustrated by Adam Hook

WAYLAND

A Day in the Life

Titles in the series

A Roman Centurion
A Tudor Criminal
A Victorian Street Seller
A World War II Evacuee

Editor: Jason Hook
Designer: Jan Sterling
Picture Research: Shelley Noronha
Production Controller: Tracy Fewtrell

First published in 1999 by Wayland Publishers Ltd,
61 Western Road, Hove, East Sussex BN3 1JD, England

Find Wayland on the Internet at http://www.wayland.co.uk

British Library Cataloguing in Publication Data
Wood, Richard, 1949–
   A Victorian street seller. – (A day in the life)
   1. Pedlars and peddling – Great Britain – History – 19th Century – Juvenile
   literature 2. Great Britain – Social conditions – 19th century – Juvenile literature
   3. Great Britain – History – Victoria, 1837–1901 – Juvenile literature
   I. Title
   941'.081

   ISBN 0 7502 2374 X

Printed and bound in Italy by EuroGrafica.

Cover picture: (foreground) the muffin seller; (background)
St Pancras Hotel and Pentonville Road, 1884, (detail) by J. O'Connor.

Picture Acknowledgements: The publishers would like to thank the following for
permission to publish their pictures: Beamish, The North of England Open Air
Museum 18; Birmingham City Libraries 19 (bottom); Bridgeman Art Library,
London 13 (top-left), /Bury Art Gallery and Museum 7 (top), /Museum of London
cover, 4, 28 (bottom), /University of Liverpool Art Gallery and Collections 29 (top);
Fotomas Index 26; Hulton Getty 5, 7 (bottom), 9, 11 (bottom), 13 (top-right), 19
(top), 20 (bottom), 21 (bottom), 22 (left), 25 (bottom), 27; Mary Evans 6 (bottom),
12 (top), 15 (top), 25 (top); Museum of London 14 (top), 28 (top); National Dairy
Council 10; National Gallery 13 (bottom); Popperfoto 14 (bottom), 23 (top); Neil
Storey 15 (bottom); Robert Opie 20 (top), 21 (top), 24; Science Museum / Science
and Society Picture Library 6 (top), 22 (right), 23 (bottom), 29 (bottom); Topham 8,
11 (top).

**All Wayland books encourage children to read and
help them improve their literacy.**

✓ The contents page, page numbers, headings and index
help locate specific pieces of information.

✓ The glossary reinforces alphabetic knowledge and
extends vocabulary.

✓ The further information section suggests other books
dealing with the same subject.

✓ Find out more about how this book is specifically
relevant to the National Literacy Strategy on page 30.

CONTENTS

Meet our Victorian street seller. Her name is Josephine, but everyone calls her Joss. She is 11 years old, and lives in a room in London with her mother and five younger brothers and sisters. Her mother needs the earnings of Joss to buy food. Joss cannot read or write, but she is good with numbers. She knows how to make a profit from selling the muffins that she buys every morning from the baker. A day in her life is long and tiring. Joss does not return home until her last muffin is sold.

The candle-clock that appears on each spread is a way of telling the time which dates back over a thousand years. It takes an hour for each ring of wax to burn down, as you will see.

THE STREET SELLER

Joss shivers as she steps out into the street. The church bell has already struck 7 o'clock. If she does not hurry to the bakery, she will be scolded and perhaps lose her job. With so many mouths to feed, her mother depends on the few shillings Joss earns each week selling muffins.

Until the 1870s, poor children did not normally attend school. Instead, many of them went out to work in fields, factories and shops. People said street selling was a good job for children. It was healthy, open-air work which did not need much education, training or strength – just a loud voice! In 1851, there were 30,000 street sellers in London. Many of them were children, and some were only 6 years old.

◀ Joss's tray is strung around her neck. Some sellers preferred to carry a basket on their heads.

▼ A street in London, painted in 1884.

'The street sellers of muffins and crumpets are for the most part boys, young men, or old men, and some of them infirm. There are girls in the trade, but very few women.' [1]

[Turn to page 31 to see who wrote the quotes in this book.]

In Victorian times, most people did not think it was wrong for poor children to work long hours. Some claimed that being poor was a punishment from God for being bad. When girls who made matches went on strike in 1888, people said it just proved how wicked they were.

▲ London match-girls who went on strike for better conditions. They made the matches which the boy on the right sold on the street.

In the 1840s, the writer Henry Mayhew set out to discover what life was like on the poorest streets. His book *London Labour and the London Poor* used people's own words to describe the filthy, rat-infested slums of the East End. Some readers were so amazed that they refused to believe it was true.

◄ These 'shoe-black' boys earned money by shining gentlemen's shoes, but some have no shoes of their own.

STREETS AND SEWERS

Joss dashes down the dim street, dodging the holes and piles of filth as best she can. 'Watch out, brat!' calls the rat-catcher, as Joss knocks against his crate. Across the road, the night-soil men emerge from a yard, with their buckets and scoops. Their stinking cart is overflowing with sewage after the night's round.

▲ A pottery beetle-trap. Without poisonous sprays, people caught and killed vermin as best they could.

Streets in the poorer parts of Victorian towns and cities were filthy, unhealthy places. Disease was carried by rats and in polluted water supplies. Until the 1880s, few towns had proper sewers. Open drains ran along the edge of the street and emptied into rivers. Rubbish was allowed to pile up in stinking heaps. The night-soil men emptied cesspits and toilet buckets after dark, to avoid flies.

◀ The rat-catcher, who used traps, sticks and dogs to kill the rats which infested many streets.

◄ This street in 1881 shows signs of improvements. The wide road has a clean pavement and is lined with trees. Road menders are at work digging up the rough cobblestone surface, perhaps to lay new underground drains.

Most people thought that disease was carried in bad air. They did not understand that the filthy state of the streets caused outbreaks of terrible diseases like cholera and typhoid fever. Some people said that if the poor chose to live in filthy conditions, better-off people should not interfere.

'The street was unpaved. Down the middle a gutter forced its way, every now and then forming pools in the holes with which the street abounded ... Women from their doors tossed household slops of every description into the gutter.' 2

A new law in 1848 allowed towns with a high death rate to appoint medical officers and sanitary inspectors. Conditions slowly began to improve. Dustmen and rubbish carters were paid to clean the streets, covered sewers were dug, and clean piped water was supplied. By 1901, many slums had been cleared and fewer people died of infectious diseases.

◄ These men are disinfecting the streets of London after an outbreak of smallpox in 1877.

THE WORKING STREET

The baker lifts out a large loaf from his oven. Out in the street, the air fills with the delicious scent of warm bread. It is 9 o'clock, and Joss has returned for a second basket of muffins. She calls out: 'Come on, mister, give us one for brekky!' The baker tosses her a burnt muffin from the cooling tray.

The Victorians did not have preservatives, so bread quickly went stale. Bakers worked through the night to have fresh buns, loaves and muffins ready for breakfast. Small muffins were 'hawked' along the street by muffin-sellers like Joss. Bakers' boys delivered the larger loaves from door to door using handcarts. Later in the day, their carts were packed with pies for lunch and cakes or scones for tea.

◀ The baker uses a long-handled 'peel' to take the loaves from the back of the brick oven.

▶ A baker's handcart.

▶ The knife-grinder's stand was like a portable workshop. He turned the grindstone with a treadle.

At night, the street was almost empty. But by morning it was filled with people making a living from passers-by. Many offered services, like the knife-grinder who sharpened knives, scissors or shears. Some hoped to earn a penny or two by mending brass pots, chopping firewood, holding horses or hailing coaches.

One glance at the people in the street showed how rich or poor they were. A silk top hat was the sign of a well-to-do professional man. He might be a customer for the shoe-black boy, with his box of wax polishes, brushes and rags. Ladies in long, fashionable dresses were certainly rich. They hailed a young crossing-sweeper to clear a path before they stepped into the road.

▲ A shoe-black boy at work in 1888. He was never short of customers, thanks to all the horse droppings in busy, town-centre streets.

'Street traders included ... public musicians with regular work, billiard makers, scene painters, travelling photographers, costermongers with a barrow and perhaps a donkey, coffee stall keepers, cats' meat men and general dealers.'[3]

DELIVERIES

Joss rings her bell so the whole road can hear. 'Muffins, fresh muffins!' she calls. Joss makes her way through quiet, residential streets away from the busy shopping centre. Hers is not the only cry. The milkman is on his rounds, his churns and billycans jangling as his cart bumps over the cobblestones.

Apart from milk and newspapers, very few things are delivered to our homes today. But in Victorian times, people could buy most groceries on their doorstep or from handcarts in the street. Larger houses had a separate 'tradesmen's entrance' round the back, where deliveries were made.

▲ A milkman's 'pram'. Customers brought jugs into the street to be filled up from the churns.

◀ Every morning, fresh milk from farms arrived at the dairy in metal churns. The dairy workers then sold it round the streets from barrows or 'prams' like these.

◀ Selling strawberries in a residential street, in 1877. There are scales and small baskets of strawberries on top of the cart. The poor pony looks even more miserable than the boy.

Some street sellers brought fresh poultry, fruit or vegetables direct from farms and market gardens on the edge of town. Each seller had his or her own cry, chanted in a sing-song voice with a very loud final word. 'Buy my fat *chickens*!' 'Sixpence a pound, fair *cherries*!' 'Buy my ropes of hard *onions*!' They cried out until they were hoarse.

'One-a-penny, two-a-penny, hot cross buns! If your daughters will not eat them, give them to your sons.

But if you haven't any of those pretty little elves, You cannot then do better than eat them all yourselves.' 4

Sellers travelled first to large, detached houses. Here, they sold their wares to servants who had instructions to choose only the best produce. The sellers went next to the rows of terraced houses, where the skilled workers and middle classes lived. Only after these people had taken their pick did the barrows reach the poorer parts of town.

◀ A family out for a stroll in a middle-class street in the 1890s.

MARKET DAY

Today is market day. Joss knows that the market sellers will want snacks, and pushes her way through the jostling crowds to reach the stalls. She stumbles into the book-seller's pitch, and three muffins spill to the ground. The puppy-seller's dogs quickly snap them up.

▲ Little books called 'penny dreadfuls' were sold at the market by travelling booksellers.

Market day completely changed the street. For a few hours, traffic was kept out and the street swarmed with shoppers hunting for bargains. Some traders, such as the puppy-seller, just stood by the roadside. He tramped to different markets until his last puppy was sold. Others, like the bookseller with his latest 'penny dreadfuls', set up stalls with flapping canvas covers.

◀ The puppy-seller. Many live animals were sold in the market.

'The dog-sellers are a sporting, trading, idling class. They love to sell and to bargain ... and boast afterwards how they 'do' a customer. 'It's not cheating, it's outwitting' expresses the code of honesty of such traders.' [5]

◀ Big city markets included Edinburgh's fruit market and London's Billingsgate fish market. Also in London was Covent Garden Market, where these women are seen selling flowers.

At a Victorian market you could buy second-hand spectacles, birds' nests, dogs' collars, rat poison, or 'beetle-wafers' for catching insects. Some traders sold cigar-ends collected from the gutter, or begging letters written for poor people to send to their rich neighbours.

The loudest, most brightly dressed traders were the 'costermongers'. They bought fruit, vegetables and other goods from the big trade markets early in the morning, then sold them from their barrows. The costermonger men wore bright, silk waistcoats, and the women had broad, straw hats. They also spoke their own slang. 'I tumble to your barrikin' meant 'I understand you'.

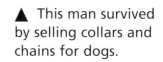

▲ This man survived by selling collars and chains for dogs.

▼ Covent Garden Market in 1864. Parts were under cover, but much of the market spilled over into the surrounding streets.

12 pm DANGER

▲ A policeman's 'bull's eye' oil lantern. Its thick lens gave a strong beam of light.

It is noon and Joss still has half her muffins to sell. Her legs ache and her head spins in the foggy street. A scruffily dressed man approaches and grasps her shoulder. 'How much you earned today, missy?' he hisses, showing his blackened teeth. Just then a policeman appears, shining a lantern through the smog, and the man vanishes into the crowd.

Joss may have had a lucky escape. The city streets could be dangerous places, especially for children. Some youngsters disappeared and were washed up by the river days later. Others were lured into bands of pickpockets, like Fagin's gang in Charles Dickens' novel *Oliver Twist*.

London's first official police force was founded in 1829, and by the 1850s most towns had a police station. Victorian police spent up to twelve hours a day 'pounding the beat'. Sometimes they had to take prisoners home overnight, padlocking them to their own beds to prevent escape. The new policemen or 'peelers' reduced thefts and violence, and by 1901 the streets were much safer.

◀ A London policeman in the uniform of the 1880s. His tall helmet was easy to spot in a crowd.

▶ Smoke from London's countless coal fires and factory chimneys combined with fog to create thick, choking smogs called 'pea-soupers'. Here, in 1872, children light the way with torches.

▲ The hokey-pokey boy sold 'licks' of Italian ice cream. This seller's cart was pulled by a goat.

There were many health hazards on Victorian streets. In 1858, hot weather caused the 'Great Stink' in London. People held cloths to their noses because of the stink of sewage from the Thames. Even a lick of a street seller's ice cream had its dangers. Everyone licked from the same glass, so infections were easily passed on.

'It was market-morning. The ground was covered, nearly ankle-deep with filth and mire; and a thick stream, perpetually rising from the reeking bodies of the cattle, and mingling with the fog, which seemed to rest upon the chimney-tops, hung heavily above.'[6]

15

1 pm THE SALES PITCH

Joss arrives at a busy street corner as 1 o'clock strikes. She sees her baker, and recognizes a number of street traders. The office clerks are having their shoes blacked before lunch. Joss hurries towards them in the hope of some business.

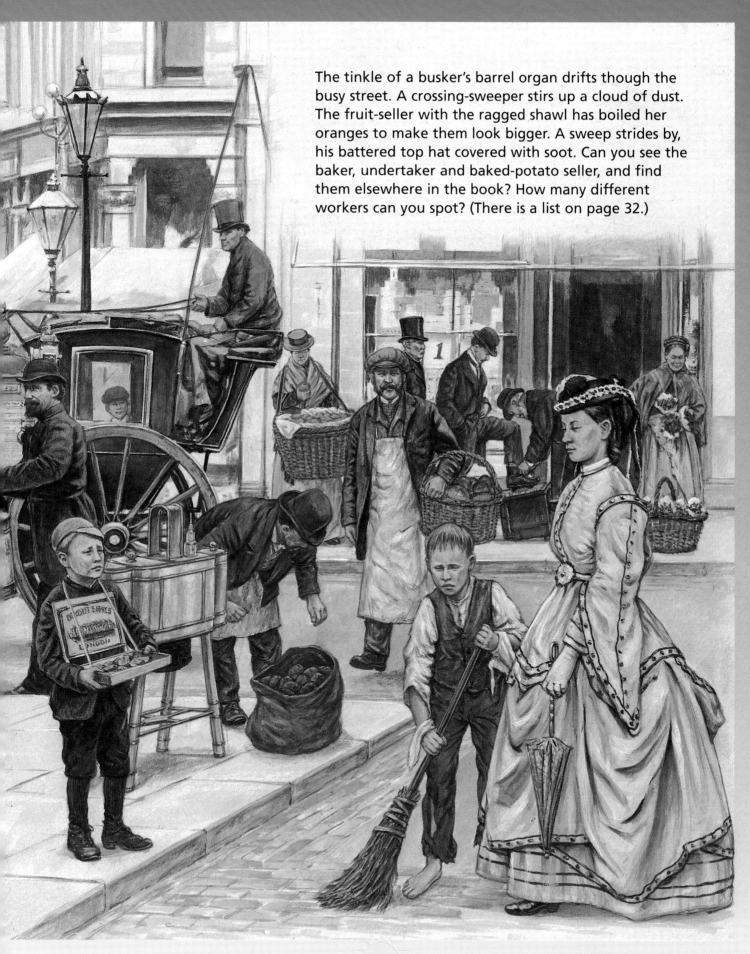

The tinkle of a busker's barrel organ drifts though the busy street. A crossing-sweeper stirs up a cloud of dust. The fruit-seller with the ragged shawl has boiled her oranges to make them look bigger. A sweep strides by, his battered top hat covered with soot. Can you see the baker, undertaker and baked-potato seller, and find them elsewhere in the book? How many different workers can you spot? (There is a list on page 32.)

A FUNERAL

As Joss hurries on her way, an eerie hush descends on the street. Four black horses approach, each with a tall plume of feathers on its head. A glass-sided hearse slowly passes, and all the traders and shoppers silently remove their hats. Joss glimpses the coffin inside, and shivers at the undertaker's grim look.

JAMES CARPENTER,
FURNISHING
UNDERTAKER,
PITT STREET
AND
9, SPRING GARDEN TERRACE,
GALLOWGATE,
NEWCASTLE-ON-TYNE.

▲ Undertakers charged according to the quality of the coffin and the number of horses being used.

In towns and cities, the death rate was very high. Solemn funeral processions winding slowly through the streets were a common sight. Poor people saved up money in 'burial clubs' to pay for a 'good send-off' when they died. Rich people were often laid to rest with elaborate ceremonies. Queen Victoria was the most famous widow. She wore black for forty years after her husband Prince Albert died.

◀ The undertaker was feared but respected. Everyone would need his services one day.

▲ A typical glass-sided hearse, used in Victorian funerals.

In 1843, Edwin Chadwick – who worked to improve conditions for the poor – discovered that even the cheapest funeral cost £5. This was about three months' wages for most poor people. For a 'respectable' funeral, the coffin was carried in a horse-drawn hearse. Although a single horse would do, richer families paid extra for two, four or even six horses.

▲ Funeral horses wore plumes of black feathers.

During a Victorian funeral procession, 'mutes' with glum-looking faces held 'wands' draped in black cloth. The 'featherman' carried a tray of waving black feathers. The undertakers themselves covered their hats with scarves of black crepe called 'weepers'. Mourners wore black gloves and hatbands, and put long, silk scarves over their shoulders.

▲ Funeral mutes were chosen for their sad faces.

'The greatest festival of all is perhaps the funeral ... the poverty of the family makes no difference to their eagerness, and the little nest egg which a man has provided to help his wife through the first months of widowhood is often lavished within a few days of his death.' 7

19

SHOPS

Joss cuts down an alley and emerges in a broad street of fashionable shops. Anyone who hawks their wares on this pavement is moved on by the police. Ladies and gentlemen are stepping down from carriages parked beneath a bright, striped canopy. Joss gazes up at the name 'Harrods' written in large letters.

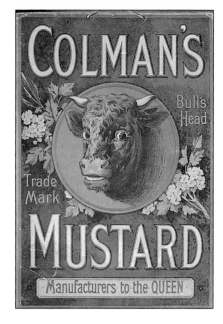

▲ Many famous products, such as Colman's Mustard, first appeared in smart Victorian shops.

By the 1870s, department stores like the Army and Navy, Whiteley's and Harrods were opening in cities. They offered a wide range of goods and services, all kept conveniently under one roof. Most would deliver goods the following day, so the shopper did not have to carry them home.

▼ The famous Harrods department store in Knightsbridge, London, as it looked in 1901.

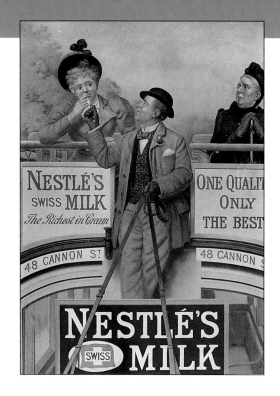

Every large town soon had its smart shops for the 'carriage trade' – people who arrived by horse and carriage. Inside, prices were not marked and it was considered bad manners to ask. The shopkeeper knew most of his customers, and sent them monthly accounts instead of taking cash.

◀ Posters advertising new, mass-produced foods and drinks appeared on buildings, buses and trams.

'Whiteley's Department Store is 'an international exhibition of the resources and products of the earth, air, flood and field, an immense display of the arts and industries of the nation and the world.' [8]

Victorian shops normally stayed open late, weekdays until 10 pm, Saturdays until midnight. Shop assistants were poorly paid and worked very long hours. They were forbidden to sit down in case it gave the customers a bad impression. A new law passed in 1886 said that people under 18 must not work more than 74 hours per week.

◀ Two shops in one. This cobbler worked from a cellar under a Soho grocer's shop. It was London's smallest shop and it used the pavement as a display counter.

5 pm AN ACCIDENT

Joss hears a loud crash and the whinny of a horse. She spins round to see a hansom cab and an omnibus locked together. The two drivers have quickly jumped down. They curse at each other and try to calm their frightened horses.

Drivers of omnibuses, cabs and carriages carried long whips to control their horses. But accidents were common in busy city centres. Horses were hard to manoeuvre in congested streets. They were easily startled by dogs, or by the honking horns of the new motor cars. Many people travelled round town by horse-drawn 'omnibus'. But after 1870 it became fashionable to ride around on another splendid new invention – the bicycle.

◄ Two omnibus drivers discuss business in 1877.

▼ Imagine trying to ride this 'penny farthing' bicycle.

◀ The Strand, a London street, in the 1890s. It is packed with hansom cabs and horse buses. Can you see all the advertisements?

As you can see from the photograph above, Victorian roads were very different from those of today. Pedestrians wander among horse-drawn omnibuses. The road has no tarmac, and is becoming muddy. In the 1890s, cars began to appear.

Some people were frightened of these noisy contraptions, so a man had to walk in front of them waving a red flag. The first speed limit was set at 4 miles per hour. In 1896, this was raised to 12 miles per hour and flags no longer had to be used.

'Looking after a motor car is child's play compared to attending a horse. If you do not use your carriage for a month, it does not cost you anything: there is no horse eating his head off in the stable.' 9

▲ An 1899 Daimler motor car. Its wheels and seats were the same as those used for horse-drawn carriages.

23

FOOD, GLORIOUS FOOD

The pieman calls out, 'Toss and win 'em!' Joss tosses a penny and cries 'Tails!' She hopes to win a twopenny meat pie in her favourite game. But the penny shows the head of Queen Victoria, and Joss loses. She wanders off to the baked-potato seller instead, to buy a 'tatie' and warm her hands.

Many people had nowhere to cook, and relied on street sellers for all their meals. Hot potatoes, eel pies, meat puddings, sweet cakes, tarts, and drinks from rice-milk to ginger beer were all sold on the street. At night, the food-sellers lit up their stalls with oil lamps, or candles stuck in turnips. Business was brisk as hungry workers started to make their way home.

◀ The baked-potato seller's oven was heated by a charcoal burner fixed underneath it.

▲ A label from a ginger-beer bottle. Bottled drinks were expensive, but safe to drink.

As well as hot snacks, people bought cold delicacies from street sellers. Oysters, crabs, mussels, whelks and other shellfish were plentiful and cheap. Fish-sellers rose early to buy them fresh from the quayside market, and sold them later from roadside barrows or stalls. Fish, especially eels, were often sold alive, flapping and leaping around in shallow bowls of water.

▶ A London oyster stall. Oysters are now very expensive, but in Victorian times they were a cheap food enjoyed by the poor.

'My crabs is caught in the sea, of course. I gets them at Billingsgate.

I never saw the sea, but it's salt water, I know. I can't say whereabouts it lays.' 10

In cold weather, street sellers sold hot tea and coffee. On hot days, they did a roaring trade in lemonade, ginger beer, sherbet and milk drinks. Popular refreshments called 'cooling drinks' were brightly coloured and had a very strange flavour.

◀ The man in the centre sold refreshing drinks of sherbet and water. The photo shows his tank of drink in the roadway at Cheapside, London, in 1900.

A tout stands outside the theatre. 'Come on there, ladies and gentlemen! See the *Bohemian Girl*. Positively the last night!' he calls. As the sun goes down, people hurry inside the theatre for the concert. In the street, there is free entertainment, and Joss rests against a lamp-post to listen to a man playing the barrel-organ.

▲ A poster advertising London musicals.

In the evenings, temporary theatres called 'penny gaffs' were often set up in shops. Members of the audience paid just a penny to be entertained with comic songs and dancing. These cheap shows were especially popular with street sellers. Outside, musicians like the organ-grinder collected money from passers-by in an old hat or tin, just like today's buskers. Many street musicians were blind or wounded, and people gave them money out of pity.

◄ The barrel-organ player or 'organ-grinder'. He turned a handle to work his instrument like a grindstone. Some people said the noise was similar, too.

'Music "hath charms to soothe", we admit. But not all music, and not at all times. Yet the street minstrelsy of today is nothing like so outrageously annoying and worrying as it was twenty years ago.' [11]

Music and words for the latest popular songs could be bought from street traders such as the long-song seller. Some street musicians played these songs well and earned a good living. Others played badly outside rich homes, until someone paid them to go away. In 1863, the Government passed a law to control the 'nuisance' caused by buskers.

Street musicians could be seen playing all manner of instruments, from penny whistles to concert harps, or pianos mounted on barrows. German brass bands toured Britain every summer. There were also Italian pipers who played while their children danced with tame monkeys.

▲ This long-song seller sold his music by the yard – three for a penny.

▶ A young Italian harpist attracts an audience on a London street in 1877.

HOMEWARD BOUND

Joss sells her last muffin to a cab driver, then hurries home on foot. She is exhausted after fifteen hours' work. Another cab passes, and the streets echo to the clip-clop of hooves on the cobblestones. Joss can make out the shapes of other hurrying figures in the pools of light under the gaslamps.

◄ A Victorian hansom cab.

Poor people like Joss travelled everywhere on foot. But the rich could travel around many towns in small horse-drawn taxis known as hansom cabs. These were named after their inventor Joseph Hansom. Two people could squeeze inside, while the driver perched on top at the back.

▼ Drivers shelter in the warmth at a London cab stand in 1888.

▲ The gaslights in Hampstead gave quite a dim light.

In early Victorian times, gas-powered street lights were being used in many towns. A lamplighter carried a long ladder from street to street every evening, lighting each lamp with a torch or match. In the mornings he returned to put the lights out. By the 1890s, some streets had electric lights. Their brightness helped to reduce crime and accidents.

◀ Lighting a street gaslamp.

'The crowded tram jogged off into the night. Young and old were squeezed and occasionally trampled under. By the dim light of two odorous oil lamps, we contemplated ... our neighbours. Half an hour afterwards we were deposited near our home.' 12

As the population grew, more people lived further from city centres. After the 1850s, many of them made their long journeys home by tram. Train services soon began running to these suburbs, and in 1863 London's first Underground line was opened.

GLOSSARY

contemplated	Studied, either with the eyes or in the mind.
hansom cab	A horse-drawn, two-seater taxi.
hawked	Sold on the street by shouting.
hokey-pokey	Italian ice-cream.
infirm	Weak, usually because of old age.
minstrelsy	A group of musicians, or the music they play.
muffins	Circular, spongy cakes, eaten toasted and buttered.
mutes	People hired to act as mourners at a funeral.
nest egg	A sum of money saved for the future.
odorous	Having a strong smell, often a foul one.
pitch	The regular site of a street seller's trade.
preservatives	Substances which stop food going bad.
residential streets	Streets of houses.
shilling	An old coin, equal to twelve pennies.
slops	Waste liquid and dirty water.
slums	Overcrowded backstreets inhabited by the poor.
smog	A thick mixture of fog and smoke or polluted air.
treadle	A foot-pedal used to power a simple machine.
undertaker	Somebody who is paid to organize burials.

Use a dictionary to find out more about the origins and meanings of some words used in this book: cholera, typhoid fever, smallpox (p. 7); billiard, costermonger (p. 9); billycans, cobblestones (p. 10); peelers (p. 14); omnibus, penny farthing (p. 22); organ-grinder (p. 26); penny whistles (p. 27).

BOOKS TO READ

Look Inside a Victorian House by R. Wood (Wayland, 1998)
The Illustrated Mayhew's London by J. Canning (Ed.) (Guild Publishing, 1986)
The Vile Victorians by T. Deary (Scholastic Publications, 1994)
Victorian Britain by A. Langley (Hamlyn, 1994)

Children can use this book to improve their literacy skills in the following ways:

 To compare the fictional opening paragraphs with the non-fiction text, noting differences in style and structure (Year 3, Term 1, non-fiction reading comprehension).

 To identify different types of text – biography, fiction, non-fiction, quotes, captions – by their content and lay-out (Year 4, Term 1, non-fiction reading comprehension).

 To use the footnoted quotes as an example of how authors record their sources (Year 5, Term 2, non-fiction reading comprehension).

 To explore the use of biography through the role of the historical character Joss (Year 6, Term 1, non-fiction reading comprehension and writing composition).

TIMELINE

1829 The first police force is established in London.
The first horse-drawn buses run in London.

1834 The hansom cab is invented by Joseph Hansom.

1838 *Oliver Twist* by Charles Dickens is published.
The first photographs are produced.

1848 A Public Health Act aims to make towns cleaner and healthier.

1851 *London Labour and the London Poor* by Henry Mayhew is published.

1852 Canterbury Hall, London's first permanent Music Hall, opens.
Postboxes are first placed on streets.

1858 Europe's first public trams begin running in Birkenhead.
Pollution of the Thames causes the 'Great Stink' in London.

1863 A law is passed to control street musicians.
The first Underground railway opens in London.

1865 Sir Joseph Bazalgette builds the first proper London sewers.

1868 The 'boneshaker' bicycle is invented.

1870 Rubber tyres are invented.

1871 The Army & Navy department store opens.

1879 Some London streets are lit by electricity.

1880 The penny farthing bicycle is invented.

1883 Women are allowed to ride on the top deck of buses for the first time.

1885 The first petrol-powered motor car is built by Daimler Benz.

1886 People under 18 are forbidden to work over 74 hours per week.
The safety bicycle is invented.

1896 The speed limit for cars is raised to 12 mph; flags are no longer required.

1901 Over 4 million people now live in London.
Coal tar is used to make smooth road surfaces for the first time.
The death of Queen Victoria.

SOURCES OF QUOTES

1. Henry Mayhew, *London Labour and the London Poor*, 1851.
2. Elizabeth Gaskell, *Mary Barton*, 1848.
3. Charles Booth, *London Life and Labour*, 1892.
4. A street seller's cry recorded in *London Labour and the London Poor*, Henry Mayhew, 1851.
5. Henry Mayhew, *London Labour and the London Poor*, 1851.
6. Charles Dickens, *Oliver Twist*, 1838.
7. Mrs Bernard Bosanquet, *Rich and Poor*, 1899.
8. 1901 newspaper report.
9. A speaker to a London meeting, quoted in *A Social History of England* by Asa Briggs.
10. Henry Mayhew, quoting a crab-seller in *London Labour and the London Poor*, 1851.
11. Article by Gilbert Guerdon in *The Strand* magazine, 1892.
12. C. Masterman, quoted in *The Victorian Age*, Peter Lane.

INDEX

Numbers in **bold** refer to pictures and captions.

The workers on pages 16–17 are (left to right) an organ-grinder, two billposters, a policeman, a dog-seller, a boy selling newspapers, a chimney sweep, a boy selling matches, a milkman, a baked-potato seller, a hansom cab driver, an orange-seller, the baker, the undertaker, a clerk having his shoes shone, a shoe-black, a crossing sweeper and a flower-seller.